Published in 2024 by Hardie Grant Explore, an imprint of Hardie Grant Publishing

Hardie Grant Explore (Melbourne)
Wurundjeri Country
Building 1, 658 Church Street
Richmond, Victoria 3121

Hardie Grant Explore (Sydney)
Gadigal Country
Level 7, 45 Jones Street
Ultimo, NSW 2007

www.hardiegrant.com/au/explore

All rights reserved. No part of this publication may be reproduced, stored in a retrieval system or transmitted in any form by any means, electronic, mechanical, photocopying, recording or otherwise, without the prior written permission of the publishers and copyright holders.

The moral rights of the author have been asserted.

Copyright text © Isaiah Firebrace 2024
Copyright illustrations © Jaelyr Biumaiwai 2024
Copyright concept and design © Hardie Grant Publishing 2024

 A catalogue record for this book is available from the National Library of Australia

Hardie Grant acknowledges the Traditional Owners of the Country on which we work, the Wurundjeri People of the Kulin Nation and the Gadigal People of the Eora Nation, and recognises their continuing connection to the land, waters and culture. We pay our respects to their Elders past and present.

For all relevant publications, Hardie Grant Explore commissions a First Nations consultant to review relevant content and provide feedback to ensure suitable language and information is included in the final book. Hardie Grant Explore also includes traditional place names and acknowledges Traditional Owners, where possible, in both the text and mapping for their publications.

Come Together Again
ISBN 9781741179019

10 9 8 7 6 5 4 3 2 1

Project editor
Amanda Louey
Editor
Irma Gold
Proofreader
Gemma Taylor
First Nations consultant
Jamil Tye, Yorta Yorta
Design
Keisha Leon
Typesetting
Kerry Cooke
Photo reference credits
p. 27: Daniel Boud; p. 30: Adrian Platt
Production manager
Simone Wall

Colour reproduction by Kerry Cooke and Splitting Image Colour Studio

Printed and bound in China by LEO Paper Products LTD.

 The paper this book is printed on is certified against the Forest Stewardship Council® Standards and other sources. FSC® promotes environmentally responsible, socially beneficial and economically viable management of the world's forests.

Aboriginal and Torres Strait Islander peoples are advised that this publication contains the names and illustrated representations of deceased people.

COME TOGETHER AGAIN

A Celebration of First Nations Music, Song and Dance

ISAIAH FIREBRACE

ILLUSTRATIONS BY JAELYN BIUMAIWAI
DESIGN BY KEISHA LEON

Hardie Grant
EXPLORE

Te, bundola nginak? Isaiah here!
That's 'Hello, how are you?' in Yorta Yorta.

I started singing when I was three years old, so music is a huge part of who I am. I have always been passionate about music and my culture, and I want to share with you how special they both are.

Together, let's dive in and learn about how music, song and dance have been so important to the oldest living culture on Earth. We'll discover everything from how to make a yidaki (didgeridoo) to playing music with a gum leaf. We'll also meet some incredible First Nations performers, and I'll share with you my own love and connection to music and to my mob.

Let's come together again and go on this incredible journey of discovery!

Big love,

Isaiah

In traditional ceremonies, like corroborees, music connects us with our ancestor spirits. Corroboree is from the Dharug word 'garaabara', spoken by First Nations People from Gadigal Country (Sydney).

Around a campfire, we sing special songs and play instruments as we dance, thank, celebrate and praise our ancestors. We also tell creation stories through dances that have sacred and important meanings.

Today, at a Welcome to Country or smoking ceremony it is also common to see people singing, dancing and playing instruments, like the yidaki and bilma. These types of performances also happen on Survival Day (26 January) and during NAIDOC Week. I feel very proud when my culture is acknowledged and respected in this way.

MUSIC

For more than 65,000 years, we have passed down stories and knowledge through song. Through music, we even share how the world began. These are called Dreaming stories.

Australia is a huge place that originally had over 250 tribes. Each tribe, mob or community has their own special Dreaming stories that are unique to their Country. I'm from Yorta Yorta Country and one of my Dreaming stories is about Biamie, the father of all creation. Biamie sent Gumuk Winga, an old woman, on a search for yams with her digging stick. When she became lost, Gane the Rainbow Serpent was called to find her. As Gane followed her digging stick trail, his enormous body carved out the landscape and the waterways of my Country.

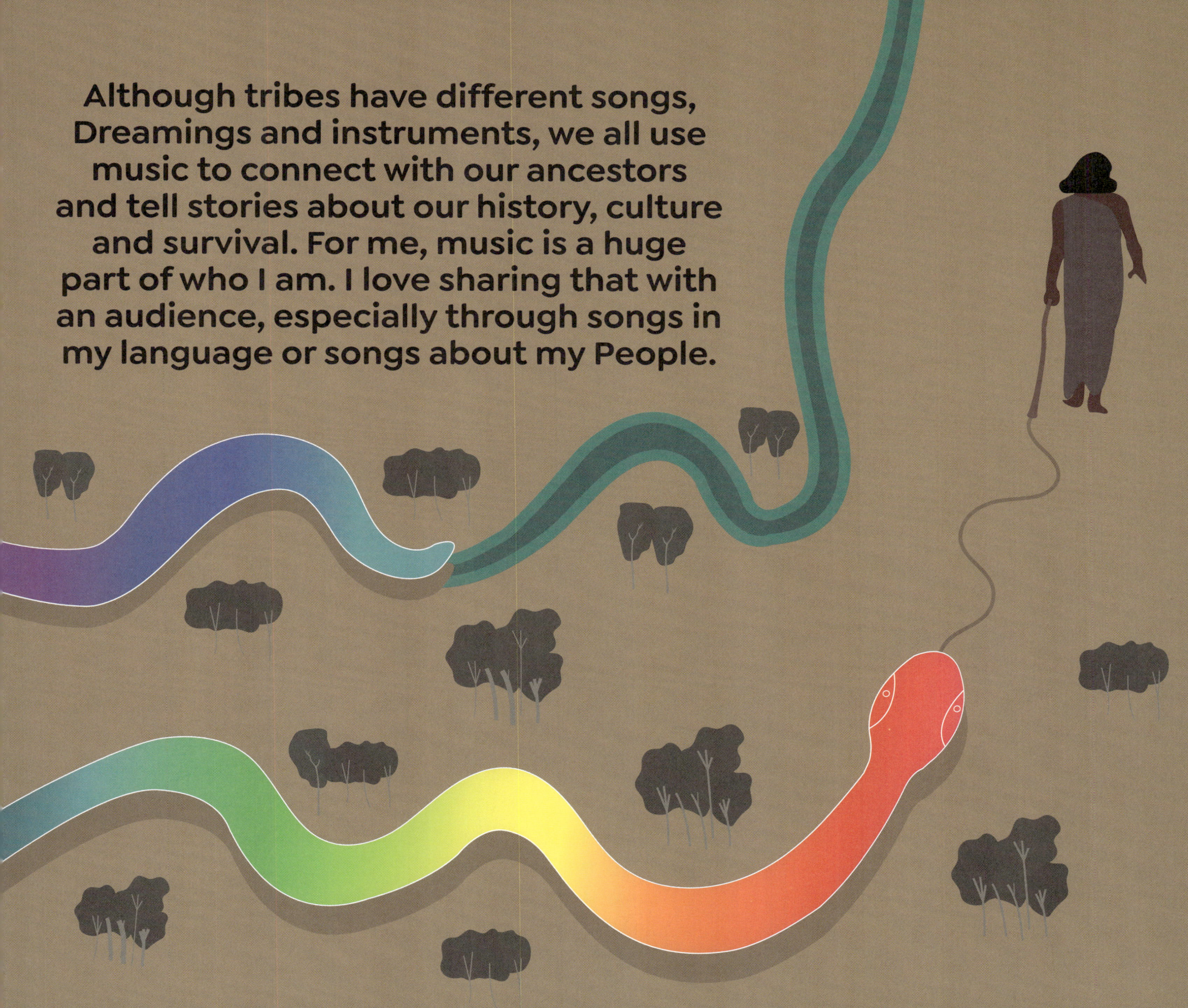

YIDAKI (DIDGERIDOO)

The yidaki is my favourite First Nations instrument. It originally comes from Yolŋu Country in East Arnhem Land and is only allowed to be played by men. Sometimes, it is played while dancing and used to create interesting movements.

People call the yidaki the 'sound of Australia' because it makes a unique, deep humming sound and can also make sounds like chattering birds, bouncing kangaroos or running emus. It's music that sounds like nature!

HOW IS IT MADE?

The yidaki is made from a eucalyptus branch that is solid on the outside. The inside is hollow, eaten away by termites. We bang the branch against the ground to clear it out, then the wood is soaked in water for many days to cure it. This protects it as it ages. Next, we clean the inside with sticks or hot coals, and strip the bark off the outside. Beeswax is spread over the mouthpiece so that it feels nice and creates a good seal with our mouth when we play it.

HOW IS IT PLAYED?

The yidaki is quite tricky to play. First, you need to learn how to do circular breathing. This means you have to breathe in through your nose while blowing air stored in your cheeks out of your mouth at the same time! It takes lots and lots of practice to get it right.

I've been lucky enough to sing on stage alongside Kalkadungu man William Barton, one of Australia's best yidaki players. It was amazing!

BILMA OR BIMLA (CLAPSTICKS)

Bilma are one of the world's oldest instruments! They look like drumsticks and make cool tapping sounds. They help keep the beat and rhythm of a song.

Bilma can be played by boys and girls, and are used in ceremonies and performances all around Australia. Traditionally, bilma were used as a tool for digging up bush tucker, like yams. They were also used as a gift, or for trade with other tribes and mob.

HOW IS IT MADE?

Bilma are made from really strong wood. Mulga trees are often used, but also ironbark, ironwood, bloodwood, acacia, black wattle or eucalyptus trees.

We take bark off branches and make them smooth with sandpaper, or by lightly burning the outer layer. Then, we sharpen both ends with an axe.

Finally, we add a coating of resin, made from plants like spinifex or grass trees, to protect the wood. Sometimes we paint the bilma with stories from Country. It's like making art on the bilma!

HOW IS IT PLAYED?

Bilma are easy to play and a lot of fun! I played my first pair of bilma at my primary school in Echuca.

Anyone can play this instrument – just clap them together! But you do need to stay on beat and keep in time. I guarantee you'll be able to pick this one up really fast!

BULLROARER

We have used the bullroarer for over 20,000 years! A string is attached to a piece of wood and swung in a circle to make a low buzzing noise that travels long distances. Only men who have been through special rituals and customs are allowed to use them during ceremonies, like burials. The sound is believed to scare away bad spirits and attract women as new wives. Women cannot use or see bullroarers.

HOW IS IT MADE?

A bullroarer is usually made using a dead tree or its branches. We use a knife or axe to carefully create the bullroarer shape. It looks like a tiny surfboard! It's important to sand this piece of wood so that it's smooth. Our ancestors used a sharp object like a knife, axe or stone.

HAND AND BODY CLAPPING

In First Nations culture we include hand and body clapping in our dances and ceremonies. Tapping our chest, forearms or legs, or clapping our hands and stomping our feet, are all ways to add movement to a performance and to keep in rhythm and time. Rhythm is in our blood!

Many songs in First Nations culture can be sung without any instruments. We can tell a story using just our voices with hand and body clapping.

LEAF WHISTLING

Guess what? You can use an eucalyptus leaf to make music! How awesome is that? Uncle Herb Patten showed off his leaf-whistling skills on *Australia's Got Talent* in 2007 to an amazed audience, but leaf whistling has been around for a very long time. Our ancestors used it to copy bird sounds while hunting, or to call kids home.

Leaf whistling became so popular that between 1977 and 1997 there was an annual Australian Gumleaf Playing Championship. People came from all over Australia to Dja Dja Wurrung Country (Maryborough) to show off their leaf-whistling talents!

HOW IS IT PLAYED?

When you hold a gum leaf to your lips and blow on it, it produces a sound like a mini trumpet. Uncle Herb Patten, who is really good at leaf whistling, also hums and whistles onto the leaf to make different sounds.

There are many ways to use the leaf. You can hold it flat against your lips or fold it. You can use your hands to hold the leaf in various ways or even play hands-free.

I have tried playing the leaf but it's not as easy as you might think! I've never been able to fold the leaf correctly to make the proper sound. But if you put in lots of practise (much more than me) maybe you can be the next leaf-whistling star!

Songs are like magical tools that help us tell stories, share our culture and have fun! Just like art and dance, they're super important for passing down knowledge and traditions.

As a Yorta Yorta man, I have a traditional song called 'Ngarra Burra Ferra', and I love singing it. My people have always had a deep bond with music. It makes me really proud to be able to share that connection with you.

Today, First Nations music comes in lots of different styles. Artists mix traditional sounds with contemporary styles in really cool ways.

Through song, Uncle Archie Roach and Uncle Kutcha Edwards tell powerful stories about history and their lives as First Nations men. They've faced tough times, but they inspire us.

Some famous musicians like Jessica Mauboy (pop), Troy Cassar-Daley (country) and Aunty Deborah Cheetham Fraillon (opera) proudly represent our culture across different singing styles.

In the 1980s, rock band Yothu Yindi used Yolŋu language in their music and rocked the charts. Beloved singer Geoffrey Gurrumul Yunupingu also sung in Yolŋu language and shared his music globally. It proves that language doesn't stop great music from connecting with people!

UNCLE KUTCHA EDWARDS

Proud Mutti Mutti, Nari Nari and Yorta Yorta man Uncle Kutcha Edwards is an award-winning musician and songman. He is known for speaking out on important First Nations issues, and singing about his family, his people and his Country. He plays an instrument called an omnichord and often performs with bilma. Uncle Kutcha has been inducted into Music Victoria's Hall of Fame.

AUNTY DEBORAH CHEETHAM FRAILLON

Yorta Yorta woman Aunty Deborah Cheetham Fraillon is an opera singer, composer and playwright. For more than 25 years her work has inspired many young actors and actresses. In 2014, she was made an Officer of the Order of Australia for her incredible work supporting First Nations performers. Aunty Deborah is an intelligent, strong and very talented leader from my community.

JESSICA MAUBOY

Jessica Mauboy is one of my favourite Aussie singers, and a proud Kuku Yalanji woman. We have performed together many times, and it has been awesome to share the stage with someone who has inspired my own musical journey. Jessica has become one of the most successful First Nations artists, with many hit records and awards.

TROY CASSAR-DALEY

Gumbaynggirr and Bundjalung man Troy Cassar-Daley is one of Australia's most successful country artists with more than 40 Golden Guitars, five ARIA Awards, three APRA Song of the Year Awards, nine Australian Indigenous Artist Awards, four CMAA Entertainer of the Year Awards and two National Indigenous Music Awards. Phew – that's a lot of awards! He is celebrated as one of our community's favourites.

MITCH TAMBO

Proud Gamilaraay man Mitch Tambo is one of Australia's most popular music recording artists and entertainers. He was discovered on *Australia's Got Talent* in 2019 and is famous for remixing well known Aussie classics into the Gamilaraay language. Mitch has performed around the world with his electrifying show. He is community-focused and always uses his voice to tell his story and inspire mob.

First Nations dance is not just about moving your body – it is a beautiful expression of who you are and where you come from.

First Nations dancers often wear colourful clothes with feathers, beads or special designs that are connected to our culture and history. We also use local plants and animal skins to make clothing. Men wear a lap-lap (grass skirt or loincloth), and on Yorta Yorta Country women wear wrist pieces made from gum leaves and emu feathers tied to grass reeds.

There are many different dances that men and women perform together, and there are also some dances that traditionally are strictly only for men or only for women. Stories about hunting or war are usually performed by men, while stories about gathering foods and looking after the home and children are usually performed by women.

Today, we mix traditional First Nations dance moves with modern styles, like hip hop and ballet. It's like adding a cool twist to old moves!

DJIRRI DJIRRI DANCERS

Djirri Djirri are an all-female Wurundjeri dance group based in Naarm (Melbourne). They tell many different stories in their dances and sing in their language, Woiwurrung. They are all connected by blood – aunties, daughters, cousins, sisters, mothers and grandmothers.

Djirri Djirri means 'willy wagtail' in Woiwurrung language. It is a small black and white bird that is known to be a spirit messenger. They were able to bring signs, messages and even warnings given to them by the ancestors.

The Djirri Djirri dancers have many dances which include imitating animals, like the emu. They have performed on television many times, including during Dreamtime at the 'G!

BANGARRA DANCE THEATRE

Bangarra started in 1989 on Gadigal Country (Sydney) and are one of Australia's leading performing arts groups. The performers are all Aboriginal and Torres Strait Islander People. Bangarra are known for their amazing shows that combine culture, dance, music and storytelling in an incredible theatrical setting.

DARREN COMPTON

Darren Compton is a proud Yugembeh–Minjunbal/Munanjali and Gamilaraay man who is an amazing dancer, yidaki player and visual artist. He has appeared on *Move It Mob Style* which mixes traditional dance with hip hop. Darren and his wife Jax Compton are the co-founders of Muggera Cultural Enterprise, a traditional dance squad that performs at many events in their communities, across the country and around the world.

ELLA HAVELKA

Ella Havelka was the first First Nations dancer to join the Australian Ballet in its 50-year history. Her journey began in Dubbo on Wiradjuri Country where she danced at a local studio, winning competitions. At just 15, she entered the Australian Ballet School. She went on to dance with Bangarra Dance Theatre for three years, before making history with the Australian Ballet.

GAJA ROSLYN WATSON

Muninjarli/Birri Gubba woman (Wirri clan) Gaja (Aunty) Roslyn Watson is a famous dancer and choreographer known all around the world. She was born in Magan-djin/Meanjin (Brisbane) and started learning classical ballet when she was around 10 years old. She has been part of many Australian ballet and contemporary dance companies, and has worked with international groups like the Dance Theatre of Harlem.

She also established her own dance company in Paris called Company Brolga. As a respected Elder, Roslyn continues to help young First Nations' dancers and strongly believes dance is a way in which cultural understandings can grow.

LOCAL PERFORMERS

Although there are plenty of famous First Nation dancers and performers, there are also many local performers who bring communities together and keep our culture thriving and growing. It's fun to get up and dance at events and ceremonies in front of family and friends. It makes you feel very proud of who you are!

TORRES STRAIT ISLANDS CULTURE

For Torres Strait Islanders, music, song and dance are a way to tell stories – performers are storytellers.

The dhari is a special headdress once worn by warriors in wars. It is a symbol of the Torres Strait Islands and is featured in the centre of their flag. Today, it is worn during dance performances and ceremonies. The dhari is tall with a black feather in the middle. It also has a line of feathers on its curved cane border, which are cut to look like fish tails.

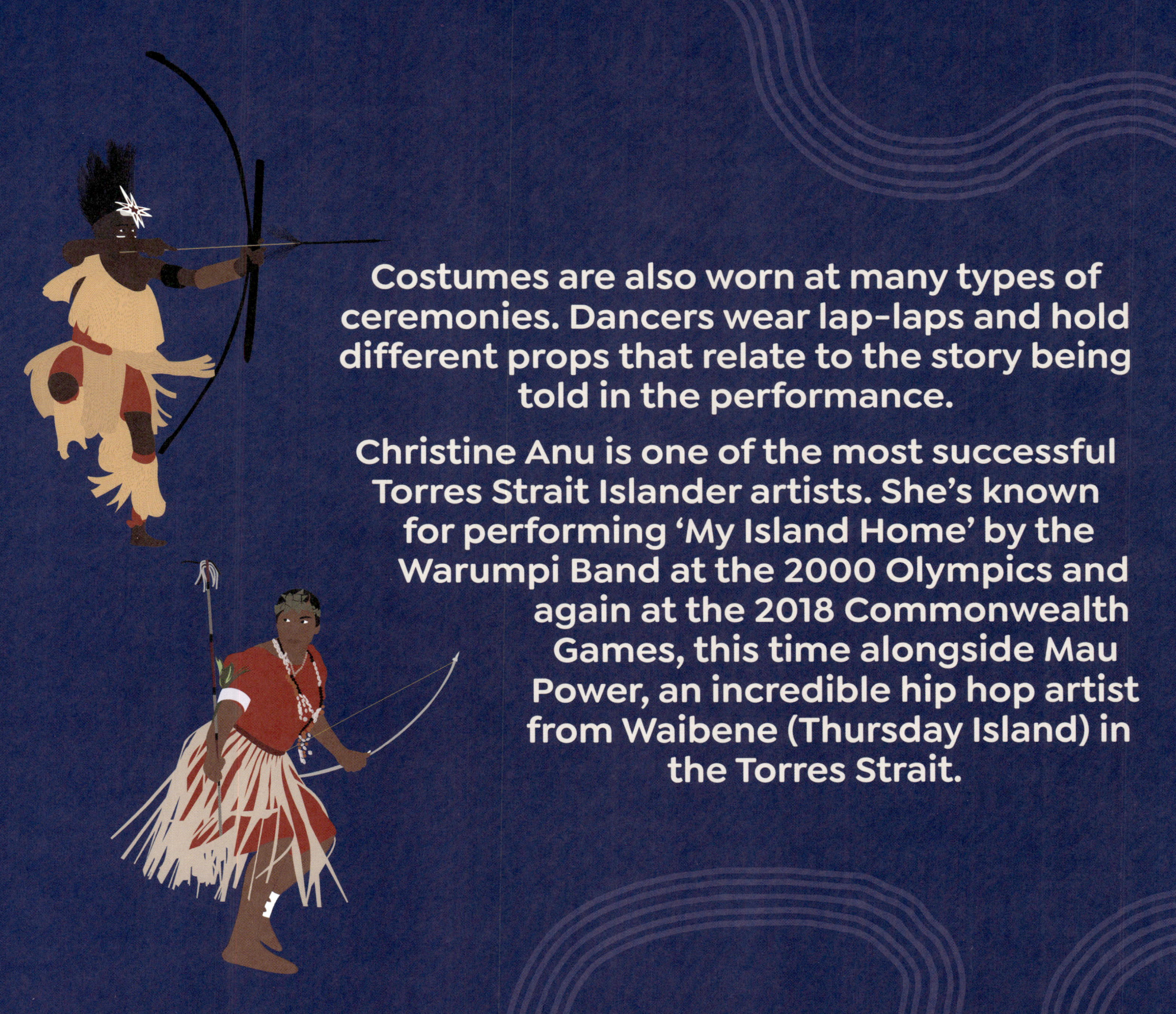

Costumes are also worn at many types of ceremonies. Dancers wear lap-laps and hold different props that relate to the story being told in the performance.

Christine Anu is one of the most successful Torres Strait Islander artists. She's known for performing 'My Island Home' by the Warumpi Band at the 2000 Olympics and again at the 2018 Commonwealth Games, this time alongside Mau Power, an incredible hip hop artist from Waibene (Thursday Island) in the Torres Strait.

WARUP

A warup is a wooden drum shaped like an hourglass. It can be played while sitting down or standing up. When hit with a full or flat hand, the warup makes a sound that is as deep as the ocean – thrumm, thrumm, thrumm.

HOW IS IT MADE?

The top of the warup is often covered with goanna skin, which is strong and won't tear. Beeswax helps to preserve the skin and to produce the unique sound of the drum. The instrument is sometimes decorated with cassowary feathers and has traditional designs carved onto its sides.

HOW IS IT PLAYED?

The warup is easy to play, and if you're like me and love the drums, you'll love playing it!

KULAP

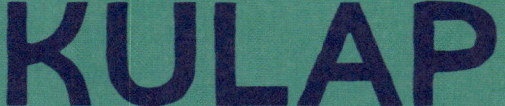

The kulap is a rattle or shaker used in performances by both women and men.

HOW IS IT MADE?

It is made from harvested matchbox beans (often known as Queensland beans). These beans are soaked, hollowed out, halved and dried. They are then woven together with string and joined to a plaited rope handle.

HOW IS IT PLAYED?

The kulap sounds like a bag of beads being shaken. Anyone can easily play these, even you! If you've ever played the tambourine or shaken the maracas, playing the kulap is just the same.

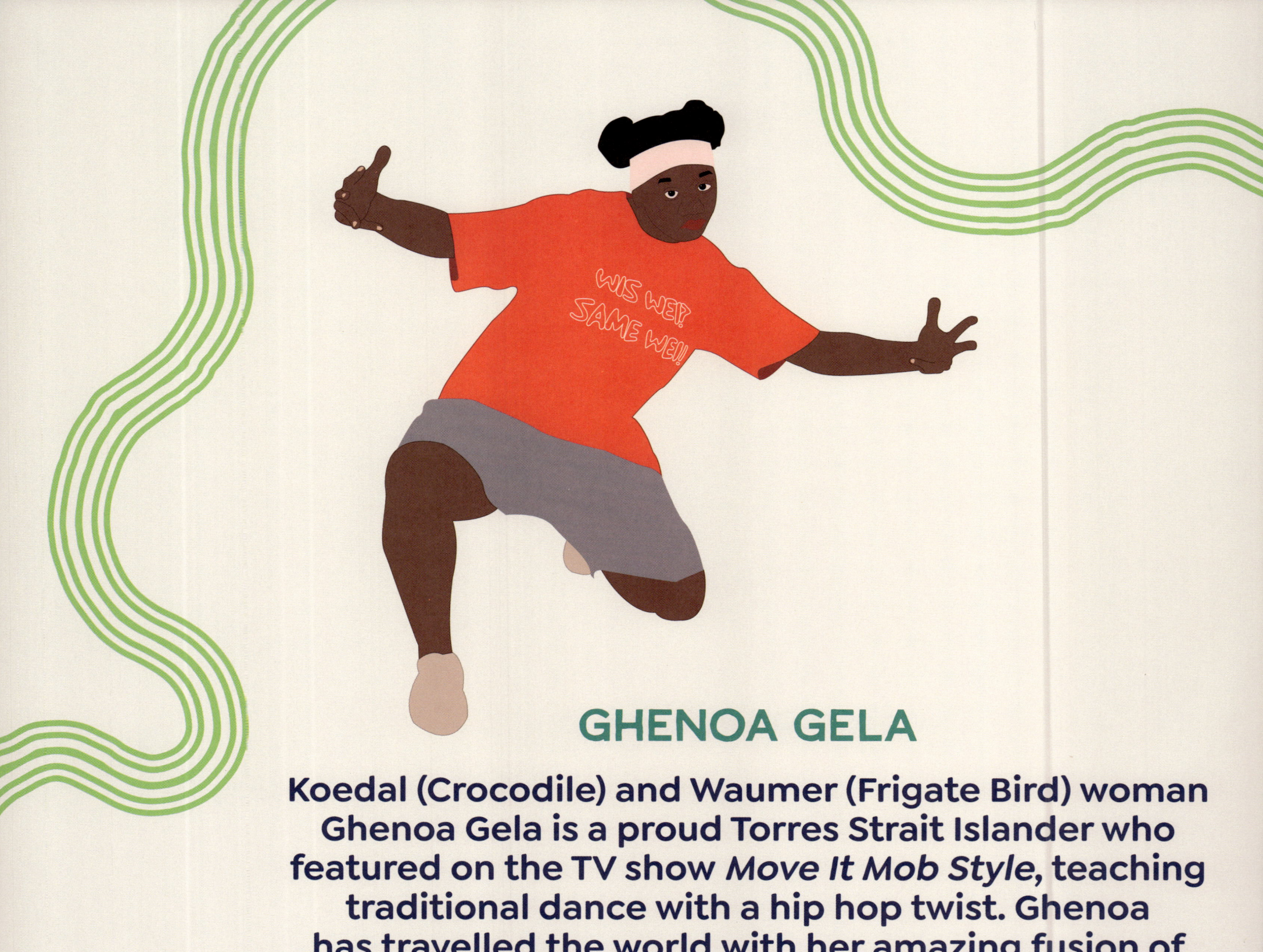

GHENOA GELA

Koedal (Crocodile) and Waumer (Frigate Bird) woman Ghenoa Gela is a proud Torres Strait Islander who featured on the TV show *Move It Mob Style*, teaching traditional dance with a hip hop twist. Ghenoa has travelled the world with her amazing fusion of traditional and contemporary dance.

SIT-DOWN DANCES

Sit-down dances are often taught to Torres Strait Islander children because they are easy to learn. Each island in the Torres Strait has their own sit-down songs and dances. Through language and movement, these tell stories of everyday activities. 'Taba Naba' is a song sung in the language of Miriam Mir. This joyful song is about going out to the reef to fish. Sit-down dances help children learn about their culture. They are also heaps of fun!

Hey, you mob! Thanks for coming on this musical learning journey with me.

Music, song and dance hold the spirit of my culture and have my heart. All are about more than what you hear and see, and it's been great to share that with you.

Thanks for taking these smalls steps with me towards the bigger goal of coming together as a country, acknowledging and respecting each other and, most importantly, learning from each other. It can all start right here.

Stay deadly!

ABOUT THE AUTHOR

Australian pop artist Isaiah Firebrace is a proud Yorta Yorta and Gunditjmara man who grew up on the banks of the Murray River. After a childhood of hardship, similarly faced by so many in First Nations communities, Isaiah's life changed completely after winning *The X Factor* in 2016. His commitment to mentoring and changing the lives of First Nations youth has seen him tour all corners of the country, speaking to young people and offering his personal story of hope and inspiration. *Come Together* and *Come Together Again* represent the next chapter in his already remarkable story.

ABOUT THE ILLUSTRATOR

Jaelyn Biumaiwai is a proud Mununjali and Fijian woman who grew up on Kombumerri Country, Gold Coast (the lands of the Yugambeh speaking people). She is a self-taught illustrator who has made a name for herself through the books *Heroes, Rebels and Innovators* by Karen Wyld and *Come Together* by Isaiah Firebrace. With a focus on First Nations and Pasifika communities, Jaelyn aims to use her talents to amplify the cultures, voices and stories from these communities.

ABOUT THE DESIGNER

Keisha Leon is an artist and designer who uses conceptual narratives to reflect her own experiences, bringing ideas to life to build connections. Keisha is a proud Waanyi and Kalkadoon woman, building her design around her connections to her continual navigation of her identity and life.